GEOMETI

NEEDLEPOINT DESIGNS

CHARTED FOR EASY USE

Carol Belanger Grafton

DOVER PUBLICATIONS, INC.
NEW YORK

Published in Canada by General Publishing
Company, Ltd., 30 Lesmill Road, Don Mills,
Toronto, Ontario.
Published in the United Kingdom by Constable
and Company, Ltd., 10 Orange Street, London
WC 2.

Geometric Needlepoint Designs is a new work,
first published by Dover Publications, Inc. in 1975.

International Standard Book Number: 0-486-23160-7
Library of Congress Catalog Card Number: 74-21225

Manufactured in the United States of America
Dover Publications, Inc.
180 Varick Street
New York, N.Y. 10014

introduction

As interest in needlepoint expands, the modern practitioner, no longer content with the traditional flowers and birds, wants imaginative designs inspired by the current abstract art scene. The designs in this book were especially created to satisfy this need. Some are originals done in the style of great modern artists, while others are adaptations of ancient, Victorian and Art Deco motifs. Many of the designs are intended to work up as optical or visual illusions, taking cunning advantage of the nature and habits of our eyes. Most of the examples, when executed in thread will conjure up a strong conviction of three-dimensionality of a very odd type. As you stare at the completed canvas, "top" and "bottom" and "in" and "out" will change places capriciously.

Abstract patterns and shapes, which do not have any built-in color associations, present a marvelous opportunity for playing with color. Since there is no right or wrong color, any combination of colors can be used to heighten the special visual effects. You can use color to point up any aspect of the design that interests you or tone down a design with a quiet and simple color scheme. The illustrations on the covers of this book will give you some idea of what can be achieved with color. Keep in mind that a canvas executed only in black and white can also be strikingly effective. Whatever approach you may use, the finished needlepoint will be uniquely your own, for no one else will have seen the design exactly as you have.

It is a good idea to work out a complete, detailed color scheme for the design before beginning a project. You may find it more convenient to put tracing paper over the design and to experiment with colors on the tracing paper. In this way the design in the book will not be ruined if you decide to change the colors.

I have not indicated how the designs might be used since I think each needlepointer will want to adapt them to his own projects, whether they be pillows, purses, belts, eyeglass cases, large wall hangings or rugs. A few designs, such as those on pages 10, 14, 18, 22, 24, 26 and 32, being actual repeats, are designed to cover large areas. However, the other designs can also be worked up to any desired size by centering the basic motif and then repeating as much of the design as is necessary to fill the remaining parts of the canvas. The tennis racket cover shown on the cover derives from the design on page 41 and is an example of this technique.

After you have decided how you want to use your design and have worked out a color scheme, the design may be transferred to the canvas. Since the designs are planned for working on a #10 needlepoint canvas—each square in the grid representing one stitch to be taken on the canvas—the design may be worked directly onto the canvas by counting off on it the same number of warp and woof squares shown in the diagram. You may prefer to outline your design on the canvas itself. Since needlepoint canvas is almost transparent, you can lay it over the designs in the book and trace the pattern directly onto the canvas. If you decide to paint your design onto the canvas, use either a non-soluble ink, acrylic paint thinned appropriately with water so as not to clog the holes in the canvas, or oil paint mixed with benzine or turpentine. Designs placed on the canvas can be colored in as an aid to the worker. Always make sure that your medium is waterproof. Felt tipped pens are very handy both for outlining or coloring in the design on the canvas, but check the labels carefully because not all felt markers are waterproof. Allow all paint to dry thoroughly before beginning any project.

There are two distinct types of needlepoint canvas, single-mesh and double-mesh. Double-mesh is woven with two horizontal and two vertical threads forming each mesh whereas single-mesh is woven with one vertical and one horizontal thread forming each mesh. Double-mesh is a very stable canvas on which the threads will stay securely in place as you work. Single-mesh canvas, which is more widely used, is a little easier on the eyes because the spaces are slightly larger.

A tapestry needle with a rounded, blunt tip and an elongated eye is used for needlepoint. The most commonly used needle for a #10 canvas is the #18 needle. The needle should clear the hole in the canvas without spreading the threads. Special yarns which have good twist and are sufficiently heavy to cover the canvas are used for needlepoint.

Although there are over a hundred different needlepoint stitches, the one that is universally considered to be "the" needlepoint stitch is the *Tent Stitch,* an even, neat stitch that always slants upward from left to right across the canvas. The stitches fit very neatly next to their neighbors and form a hard finish with the distinctive look that belongs to needlepoint. The three most familiar variations of Tent Stitch are: Plain Half-Cross Stitch, Continental Stitch and Basket Weave or Diagonal Stitch. The choice of stitch has a great deal to do with the durability of the finished product.

Plain Half-Cross Stitch, while it does not cover the canvas as well as the other two variations, provides the most economical use of yarn. It uses about one yard of yarn for a square inch of canvas. The stitch works up quickly, but it has a tendency to pull out of shape, a disadvantage that can be corrected in blocking. This stitch should only be used for pictures, wall hangings and areas that will receive little wear. It must be worked on a double-mesh canvas.

Continental Stitch, since it covers the front and back of the canvas, requires more wool than the Plain Half-Cross Stitch (it uses about 1¼ yards of yarn to cover a square inch of fabric). The stitch works up with more thickness on the back than on the front. As a result the piece is more attractive with better

wearing ability. This is an ideal stitch for tote bags, belts, headbands, upholstery and rugs since the padding on the reverse saves wear on the needlepoint. The Continental Stitch also pulls the canvas out of shape, but this is easily corrected by blocking.

The Basket Weave or Diagonal Stitch makes an article that is very well padded and will wear well. It uses the same amount of wool as the Continental Stitch and does not pull the canvas out of shape. Since the stitch is actually woven into the canvas, it reinforces the back. This stitch is especially suited for needlepoint projects that will receive a great deal of wear, such as chair seats and rugs. Its disadvantage is that it lacks maneuverability and is hard to do in areas where there are small shapes or intricate designs.

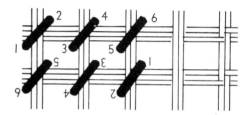

Plain Half-Cross Stitch: Always work Half-Cross Stitch from left to right, then turn the canvas around and work the return row, still stitching from left to right. Bring the needle to the front of the canvas at a point that will be the bottom of the first stitch. The needle is in a vertical position when making the stitch. Keep the stitches loose for minimum distortion and good coverage.

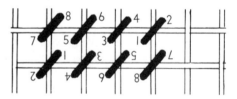

Continental Stitch: Start this design at the upper right-hand corner and work from right to left. The needle is slanted and always brought out a mesh ahead. The resulting stitch is actually a Half-Cross Stitch on top and a slanting stitch on the back. When the row is finished, turn the canvas around and work the return row, still stitching from right to left.

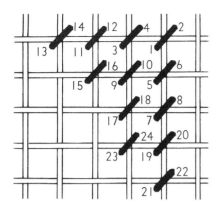

Basket Weave or Diagonal Stitch: Start the Basket Weave in the top right-hand corner *(left-handed workers should begin at the lower left)*. Work the rows diagonally from left to right and then up the canvas from right to left. The rows must be alternated properly or a faint ridge will show where the pattern has been interrupted. Always stop working in the middle of a row rather than at the end so you will know in what direction your are working.

When starting a project, allow at least a 2″ margin of plain canvas around the needlepoint. Bind all the raw edges of the canvas with masking tape, double-fold bias tape or even adhesive tape. There are no set rules on where to begin a design. Generally it is easier to begin close to the center and work outward toward the edges of the canvas, working the backgrounds or borders last. To avoid fraying the yarn, work with strands not longer than 18″.

When you have finished your needlepoint, it should be blocked. No matter how straight you have kept your work, blocking will give it a professional look.

Any hard, flat surface that you do not mind marring with nail holes and one that will not be warped by wet needlepoint can serve as a blocking board. A large piece of plywood, an old drawing board or an old-fashioned doily blocker are ideal.

Moisten a Turkish towel in cold water and roll the needlepoint in the towel. Leaving the needlepoint in the towel overnight will insure that both the canvas and the yarn are thoroughly and evenly dampened. Do not saturate the needlepoint! Never hold the needlepoint under the faucet as this much water is not necessary.

Mark the desired outline on the blocking board, making sure that the corners are straight. Lay the needlepoint on the blocking board, and tack the canvas with thumbtacks about ½″ to ¾″ apart. It will probably take a good deal of pulling and tugging to get the needlepoint straight, but do not be afraid of this stress. Leave the canvas on the blocking board until thoroughly dry. Never put an iron on your needlepoint. You cannot successfully block with a steam iron because the needlepoint must dry in the straightened position. You may also have needlepoint blocked professionally. If you have a pillow made, a picture framed, or chair seat mounted, the craftsman may include the blocking in his price.

Your local needlepoint shop or department where you buy your materials will be happy to help you with any problems.

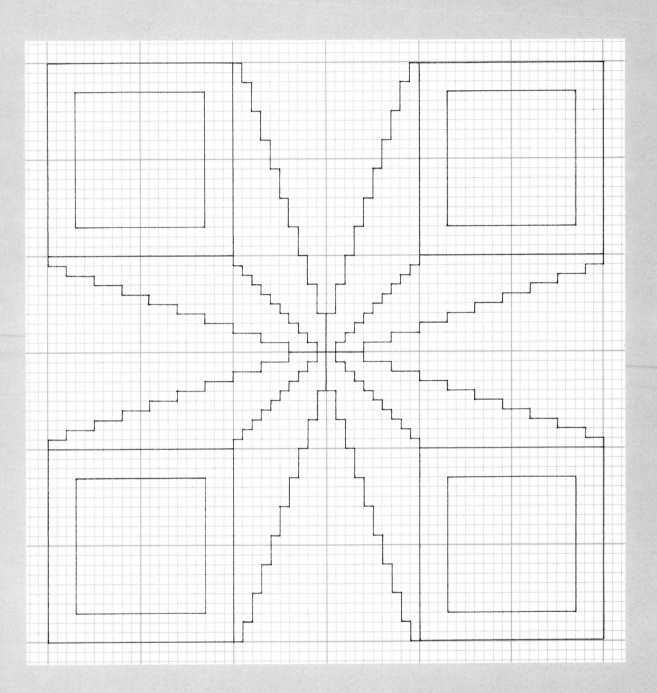

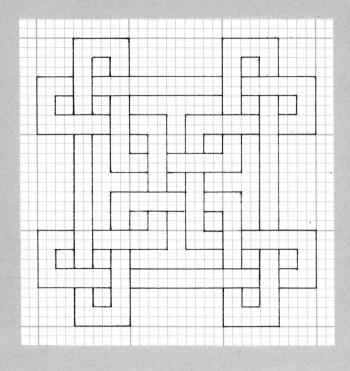

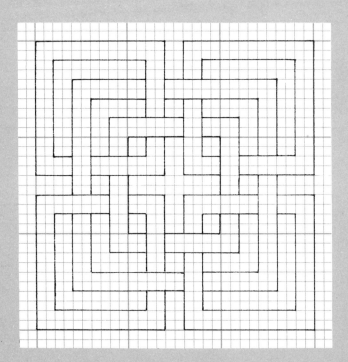

2

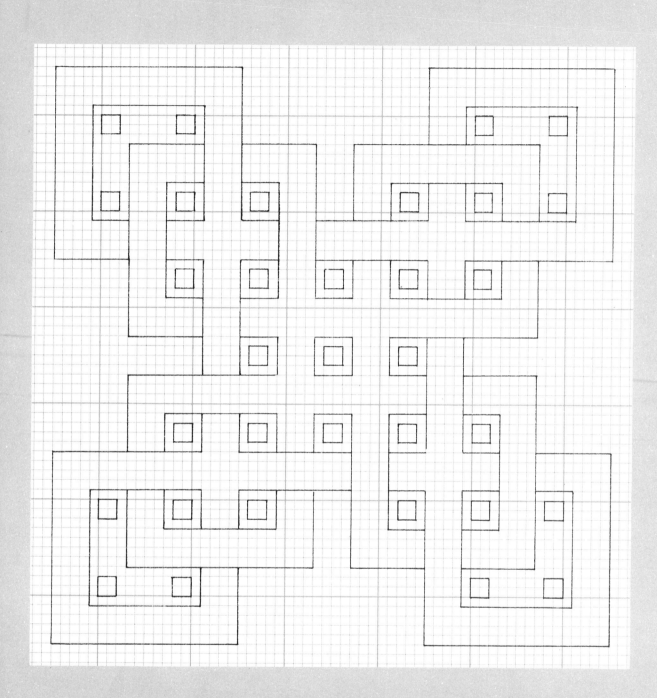

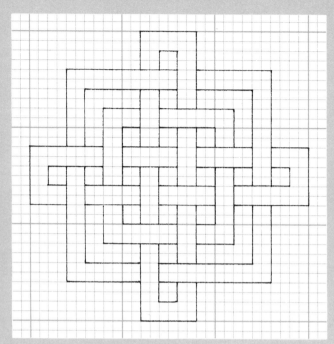

Appears in color on inside back cover.

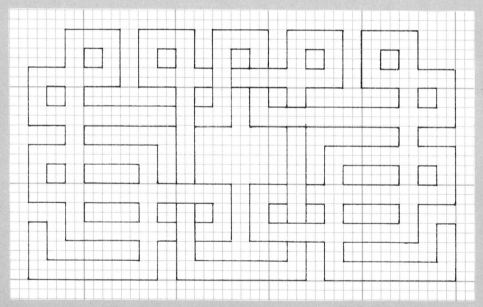

Appears in color on inside back cover.

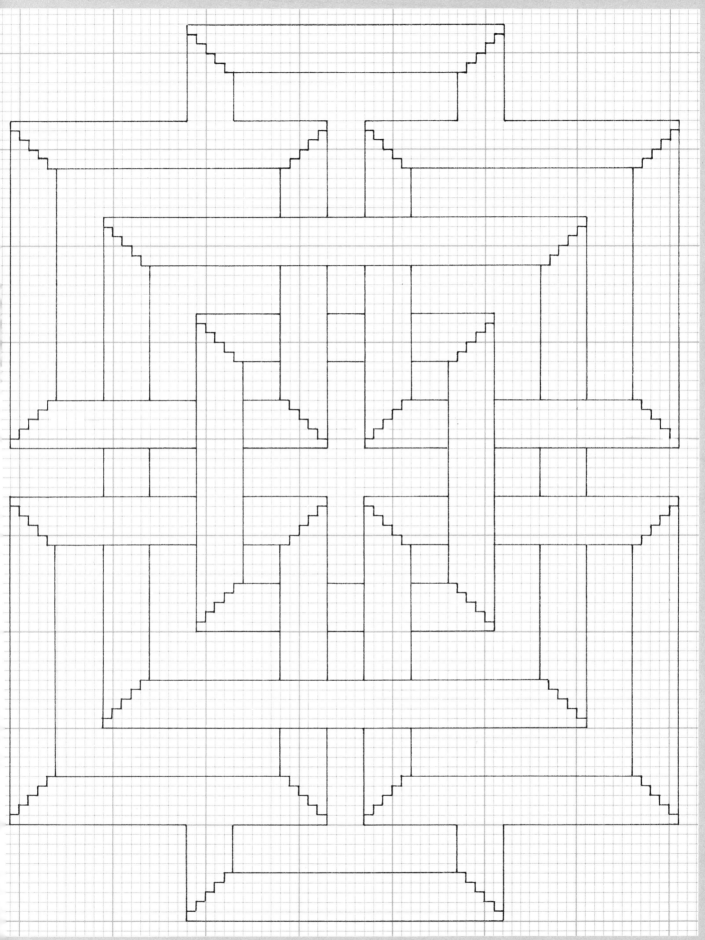

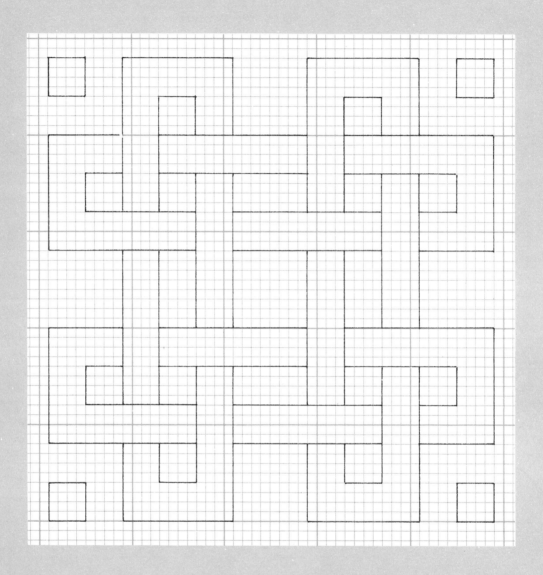

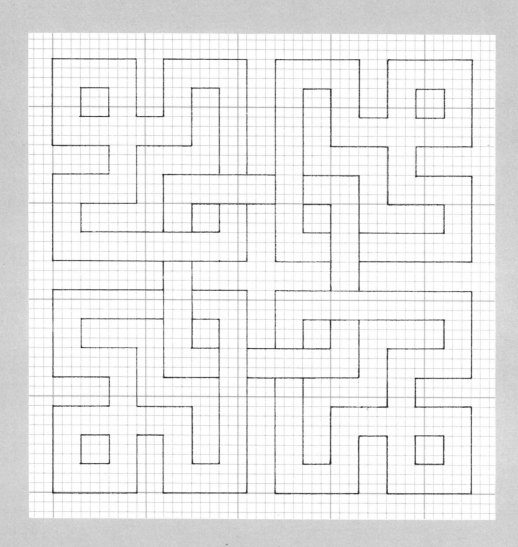

8

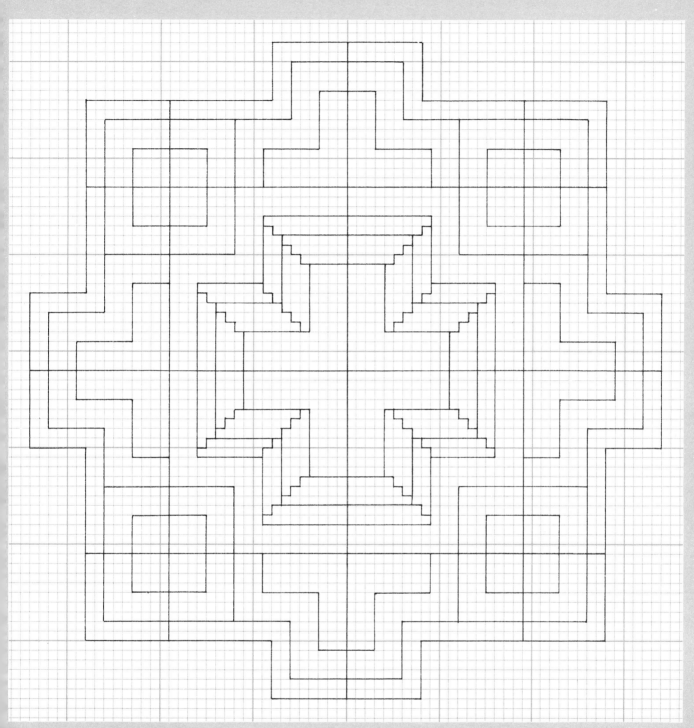

Appears in color on back cover.

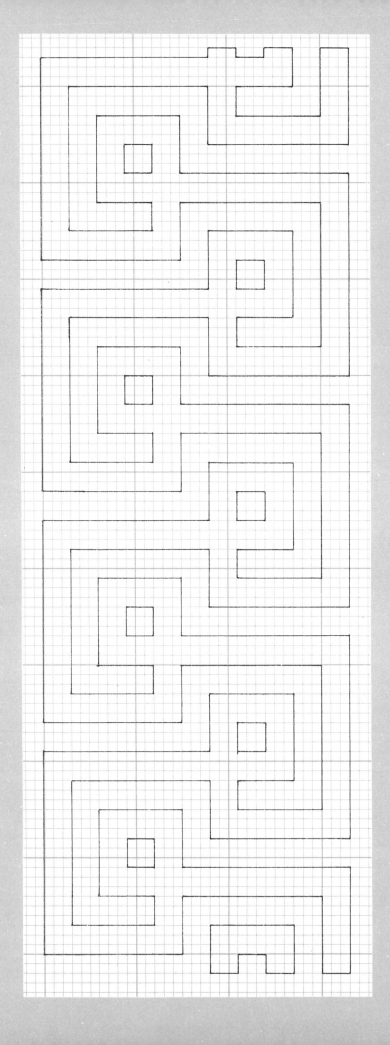

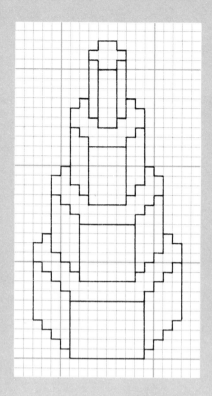

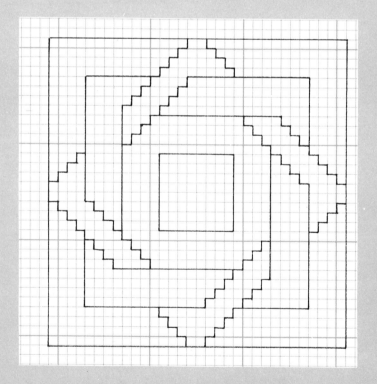

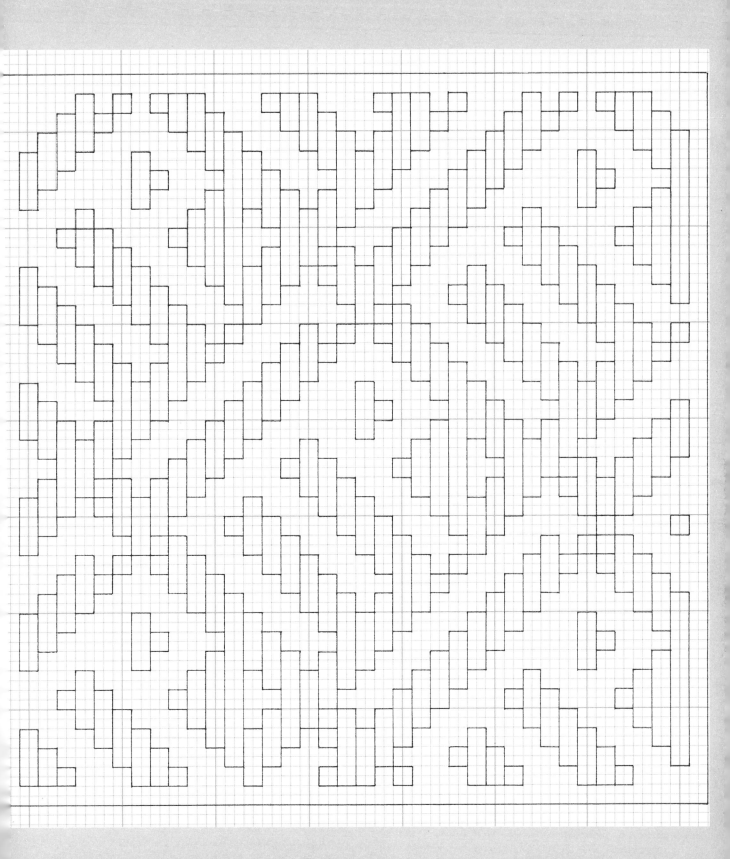

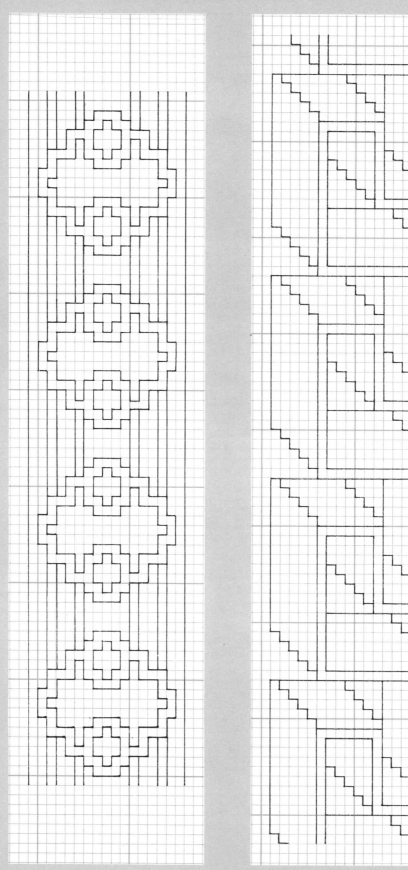

Appears in color on inside back cover.

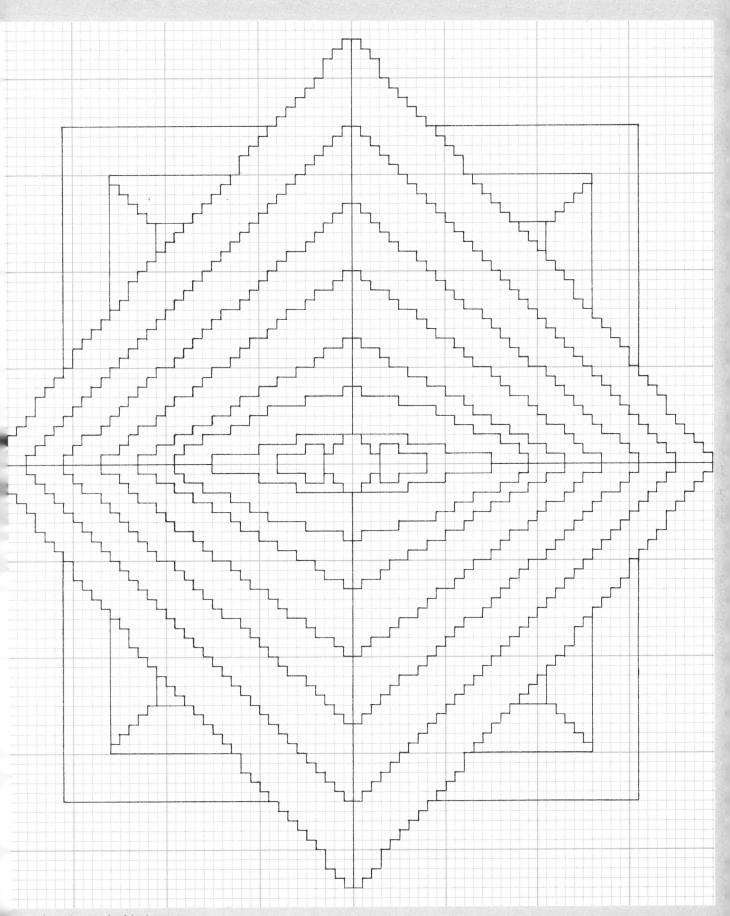

ears in color on inside front cover.

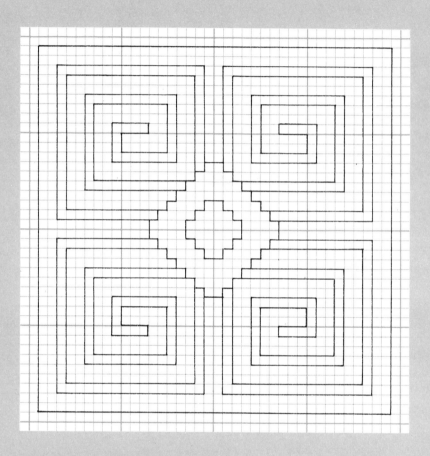

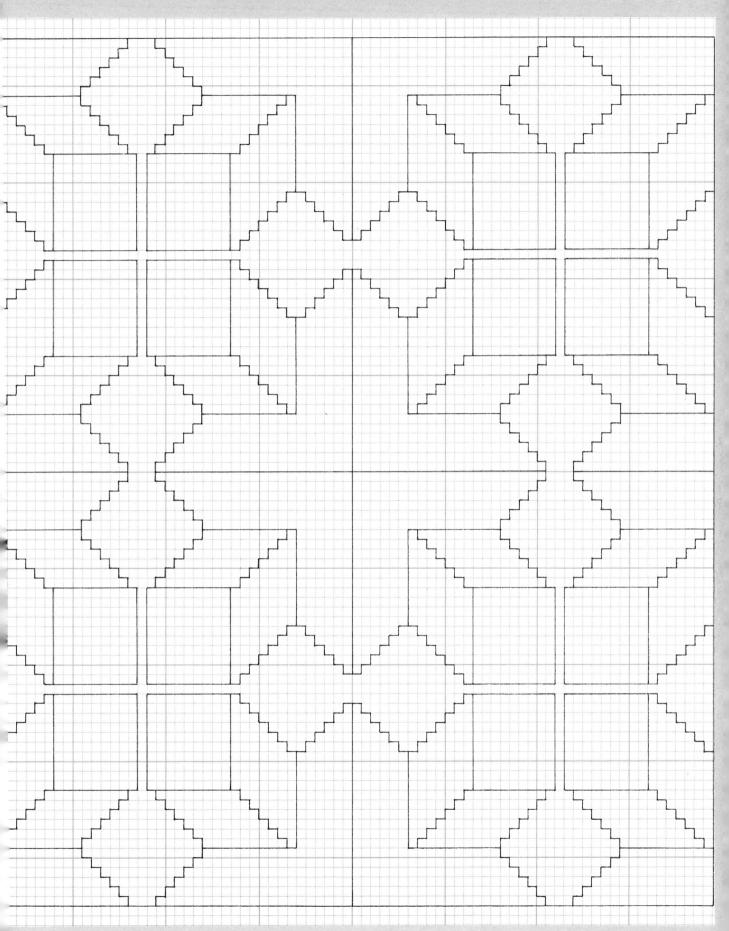

ears in color on back cover.

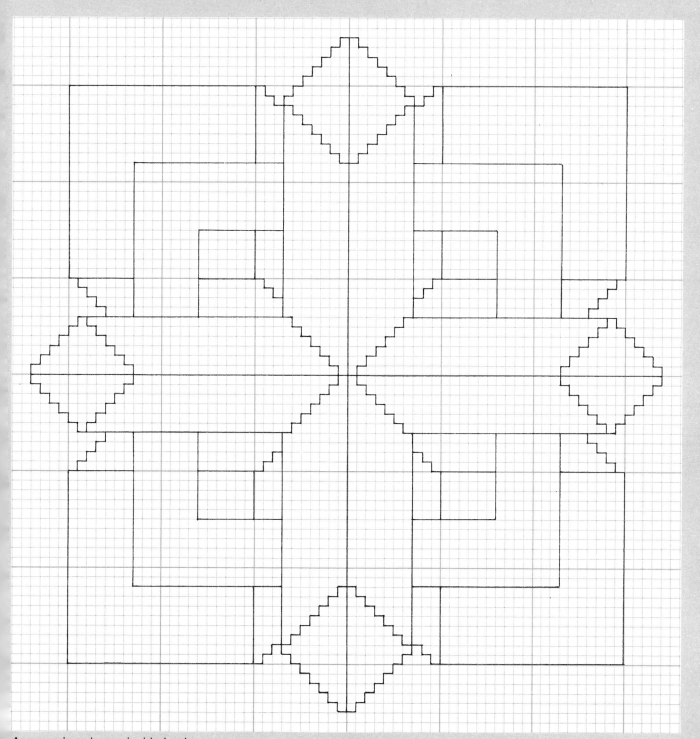

Appears in color on inside back cover.

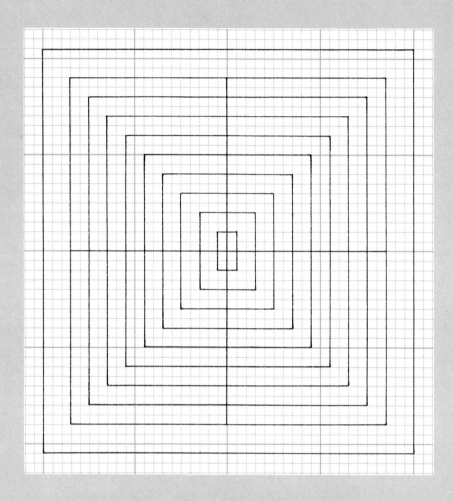

Appears in color on back cover.

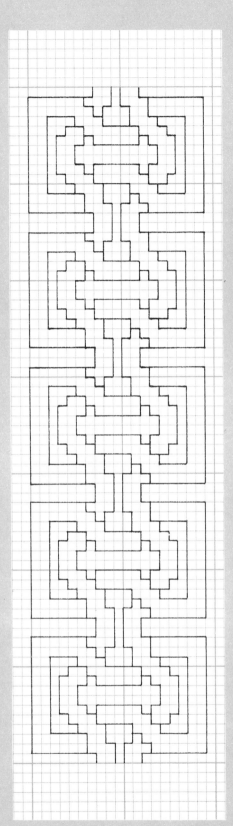

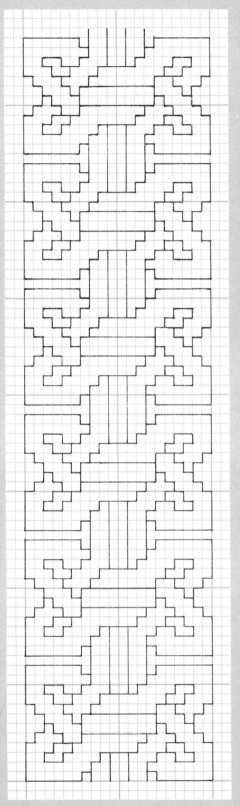

Appears in color on inside front cover. Appears in color on inside back cover.

Appears in color on inside front cover.

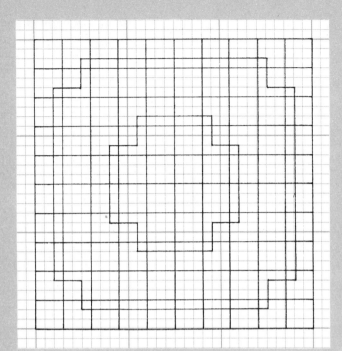

Appears in color on inside back cover.

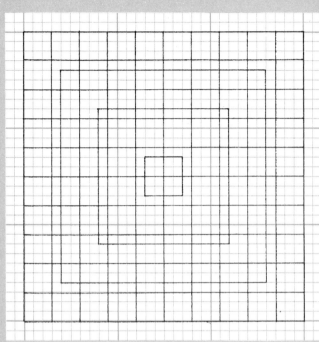

Appears in color on inside back cover.

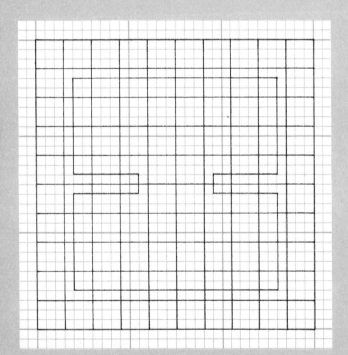

Appears in color on inside back cover.

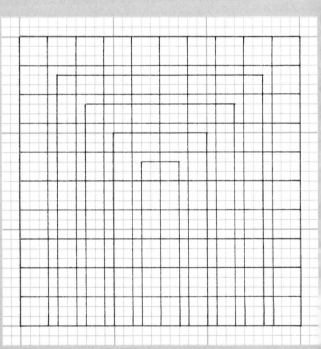

Appears in color on inside back cover.

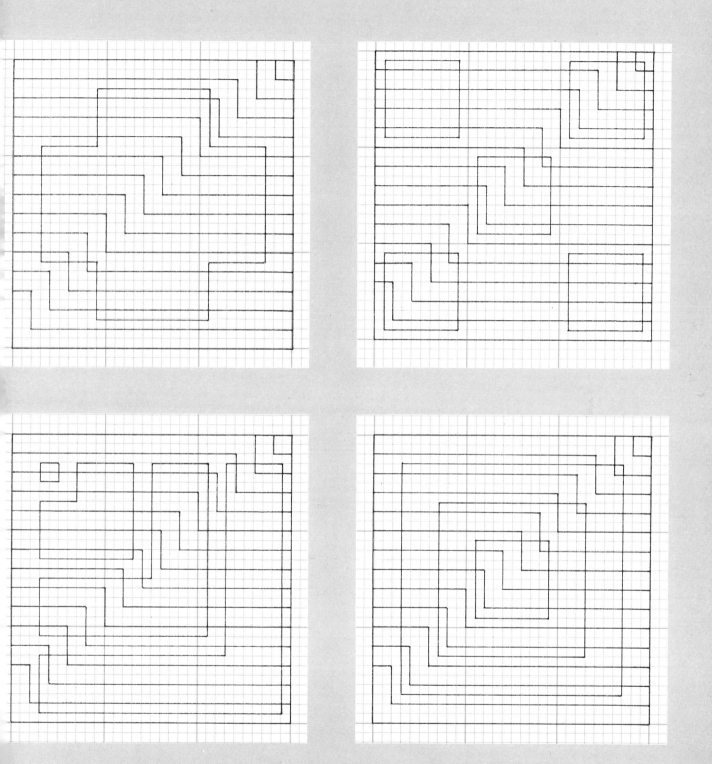

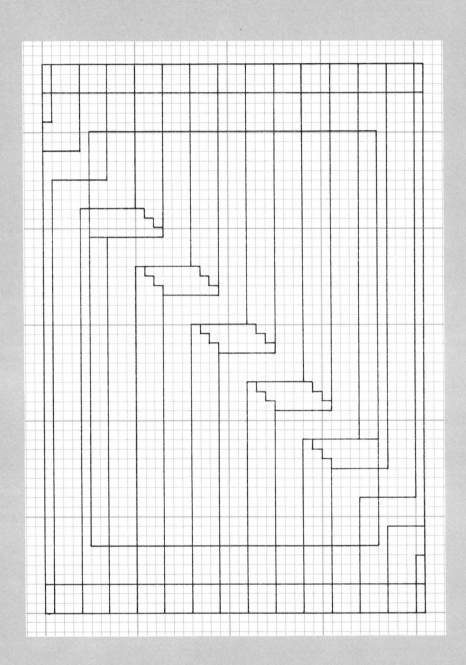

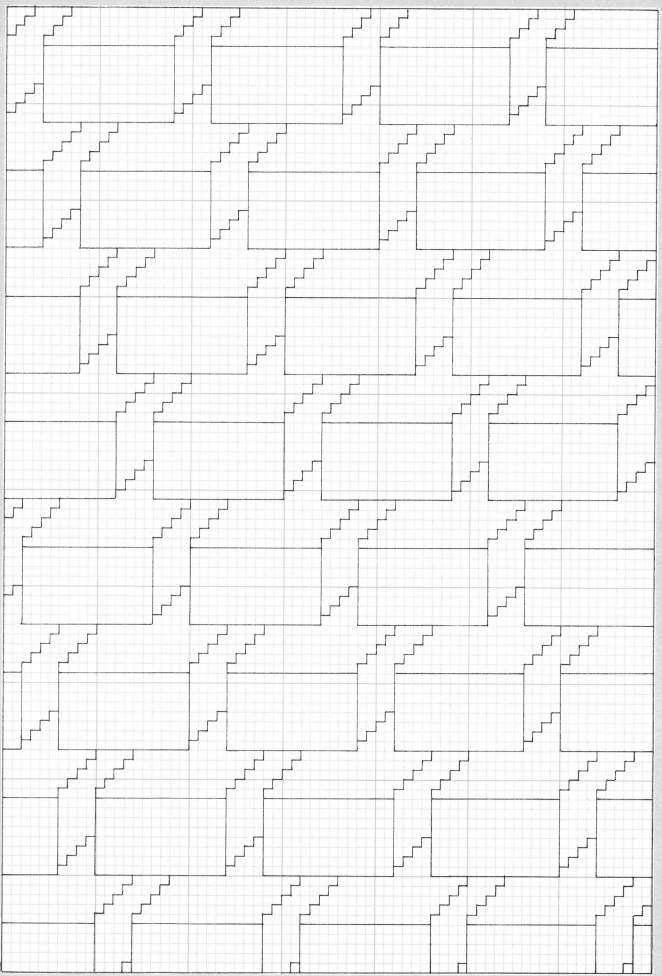

Appears in color on inside front cover.

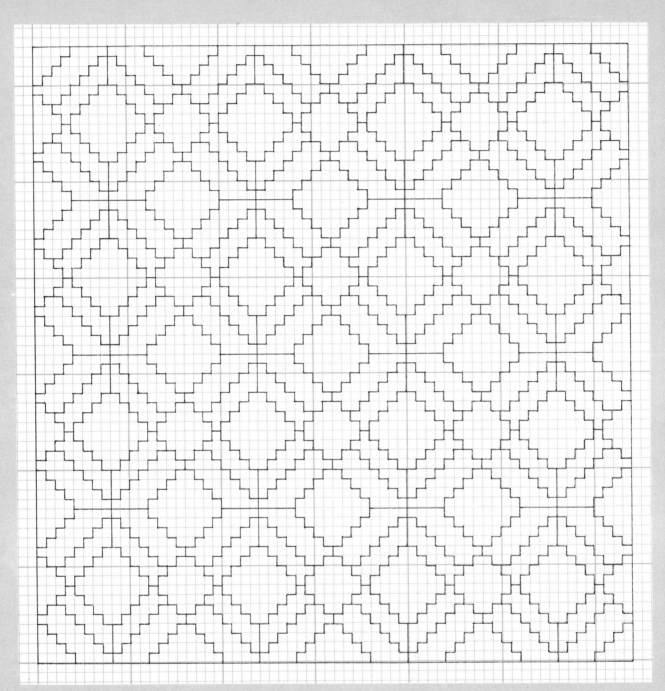

Appears in color on inside back cover.

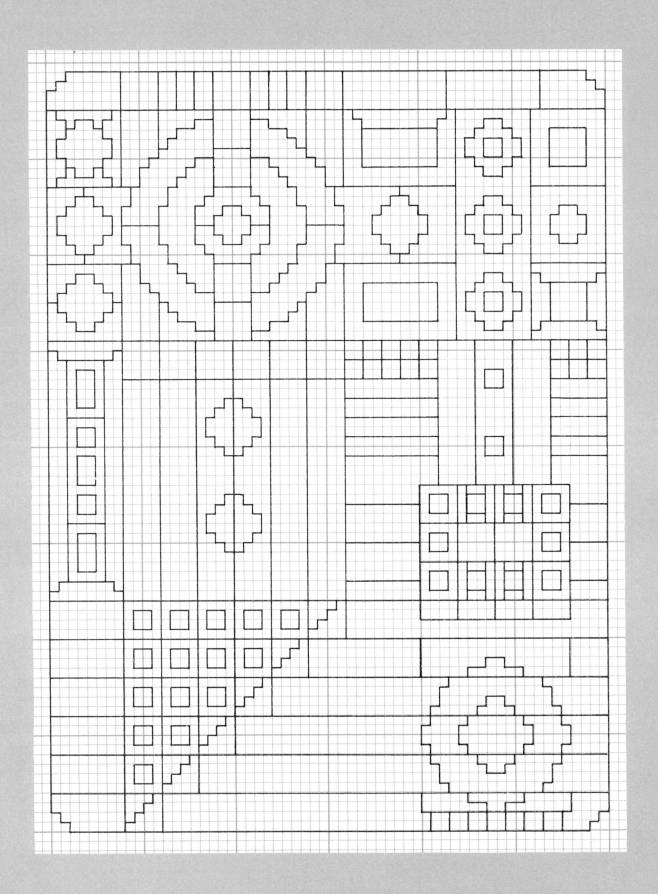

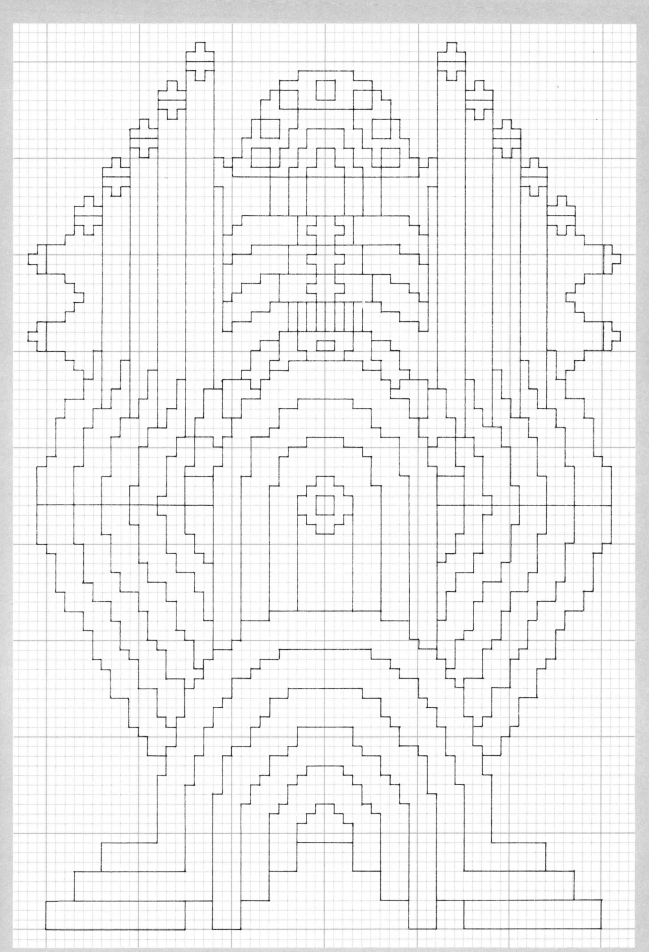

Appears in color on inside back cover.

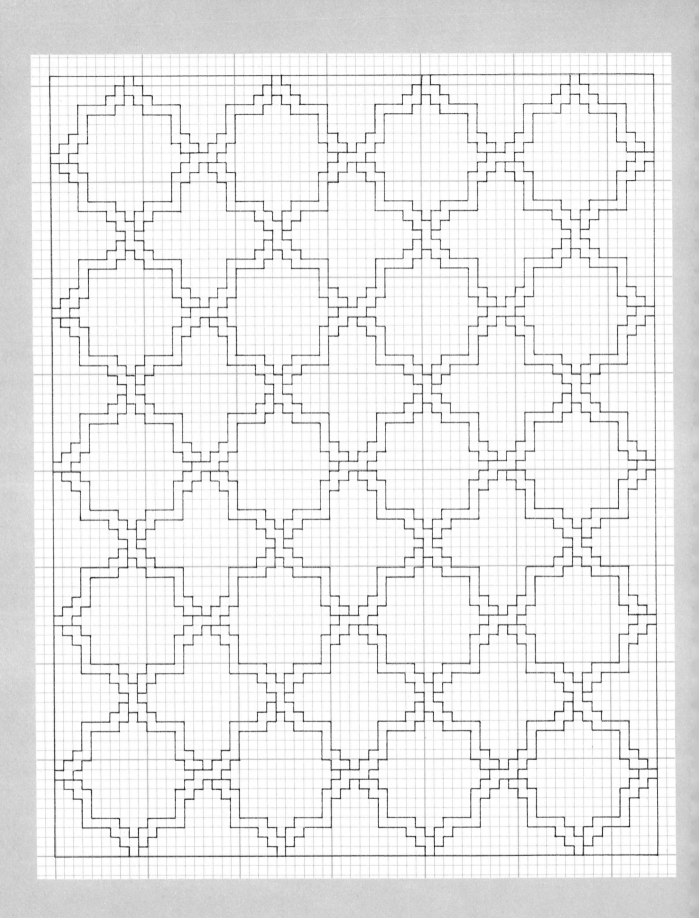

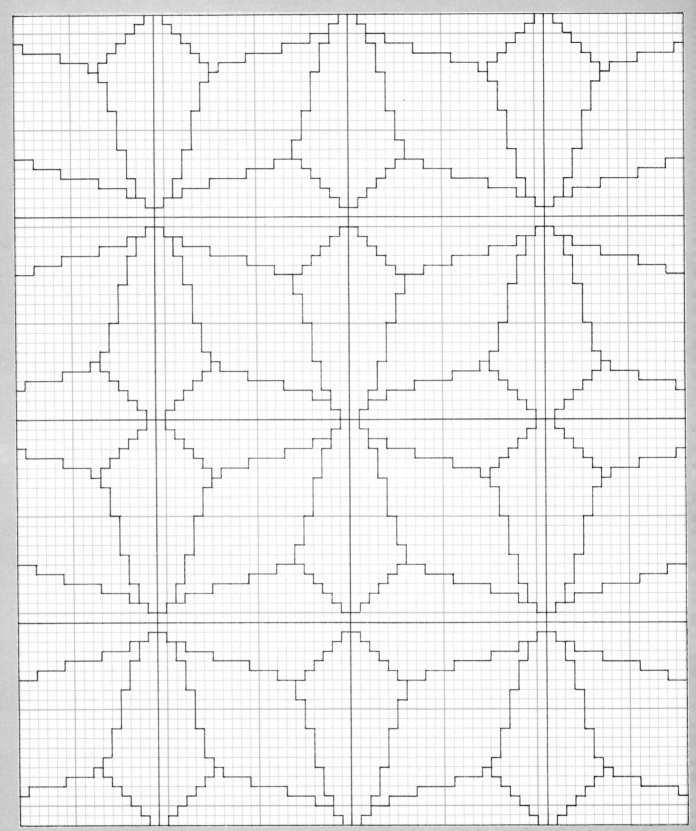

Appears in color on inside front cover.

dered in needlepoint on front cover.